LEONARD ABRAM

WEBSITE ADVERTISING

The Ultimate Guide on Website Advertising, Discover the Effective Strategies on How to Increase Your Website Traffic Through Advertising and Promotion

Descrierea CIP a Bibliotecii Naționale a României
LEONARD ABRAM
   WEBSITE ADVERTISING. The Ultimate Guide on Website Advertising, Discover the Effective Strategies on How to Increase Your Website Traffic Through Advertising and Promotion / Leonard Abram – Bucharest: Editura My Ebook, 2021
   ISBN

LEONARD ABRAM

WEBSITE ADVERTISING

The Ultimate Guide on Website Advertising, Discover the Effective Strategies on How to Increase Your Website Traffic Through Advertising and Promotion

My Ebook Publishing House
Bucharest, 2021

CONTENTS

So You Want to Use Your Website to Generate Revenue	7
Website Advertising Drives Results	9
A Closer Look at The Banner Ad	12
Different Web Ads Serve Different Purposes	14
How To Create An Effective Banner Ad	17
What To Look For In Sites Where You Want to Advertise	19
What's Up Next for Advertising on the Web	22
Selling Ad Space on the Web	25
A Run-Down of the Types of Web-based Ads	27
Buying and Selling Web-based Advertising	30
Banner Ads Vs Other Types of Ads	32
The Web All Advertising All the Time	34
The Evolution of Web-based Advertising	36
Different Web Ads Serve Different Purposes	39

Website Ads Comes in Different Shapes and Sizes	42
Defining the Objectives of a Banner Ad	45
Buying Advertising Space on the Web	48
Know Your Options for Web Based Ads	51
Introducing Television Commercials to the Web	53
A Short History of A Bold Media	56
Website Advertising's Brief History Includes Rapid Evolutions	59
How the Web Reinvigorated Advertising	62
Website Advertising Continuing to Evolve	64
The Future of Website Advertising	67

SO YOU WANT TO USE YOUR WEBSITE TO GENERATE REVENUE

Many people who would otherwise never have dreamed of being in business for themselves have found that the web has helped them do just that. And for everyone of these cases, there is another case of someone who has started a blog and wants to generate a little side cash by selling advertising on it. If you are in either of these camps, there is some good basic advice to follow about how to get started. Selling advertising on the web is not a cake walk, but it is also achievable.

One of the great advantages of the web is that it is a highly targeted media form, so when you are looking to sell space, and you have a site that appeals to a sought after niche, you have a great advantage. Advertisers will pay a premium for those site that offer access to some of these narrow niches. However, this is not to say that overall traffic levels are not important, they are, but it is encouraging to know that having a smaller following amongst a prize group of potential buyers is also attractive to ad buyers.

Still, selling ad space does require some planning and success will be easier to attention by following some simple steps. For those just starting out, take a look at the idea of joining a banner ad network. Banner ad networks undertake the work of attracting advertisers. After the ads are brokered, banner ad networks then take on the role of monitoring the success of the ads in addition to helping you find the right placement of ads on your site.

You can also consider selling the any space on your own, and many people who have sights that are sufficiently trafficked do just this. Advertisers are in the driver's seat when it comes to calling the shots because there are fewer of them than there are of web sites. So, you will need to present your traffic numbers as well as any information on marketing or other steps you are taking to keep traffic to your site robust. You can use your size to your advantage if you are willing to be flexible on price. Brand name advertisers might be enticed to your site if they can get a better rate, so even if you have to reduce rates a little to do so, getting the bigger advertisers will help to convince other advertisers of the value of your site.

WEBSITE ADVERTISING DRIVES RESULTS

When advertising was first brought to the web, many people said that it would never catch on as a dominant form of advertising. While early adopters saw great promise in the web as an ad delivery vehicle, many people thought that either there would never been enough users to justify the ads or that the use of advertising on the web would not be accepted by viewers. About ten years later, many of the newspapers and magazines that once dominated has advertising vehicles were no longer in business, and the major news organizations were suffering financially.

In between those two periods, advertising migrated to the web, and today web based advertising is the fastest growing segment of the advertising world. This trend has been in play for several years, and shows no signs of slowing. And there are some very compelling reasons why this should continue to be the case.

Advertisers use the web in several ways, but primarily they are looking to achieve one or more a few different aims. First, there is branding. Branding is a traditional form of advertising that seeks to form a particular association to a company and/or its products and services. When branding is the dominate aim of advertising, you tend to see just the product or company name, and then some time of image or text. Some common forms of branding occur when, for example, a golf club maker pays a PGA pro to sew its logo on his shirt sleeve.

Branding then is contrasted with direct response advertising, which is the form most web ads take. Direct response advertising seeks to do what it name suggests; namely is seeks to create a response on the part of the viewer. Specifically, web ads seek to drive viewers to either immediately buy a product, or obtain additional information about a product. Some forms of direct response ads lead viewers to click on a link that well provide them a download that is relevant to the product or services, for example a survey that provides information about business needs the advertisers consults on.

Web based ads have become tremendously popular, and many advertisers are shifting ever larger portions of their ad budgets to this outlet. As the underlying technology that allows ads to be targeted to viewers' interests, likely even more dollars will be poured into web ads. What remains to be seen is how much more invasive web ads will become into the viewer experience of the web.

A CLOSER LOOK AT THE BANNER AD

There are many different types of ads seen on the web these days, and they all share a common ancestor: the banner ad. While the variation in the web ads has evolved very rapidly in the past few years, and now includes everything from the traditional banner ad to the "television ad," it is the banner ad that is still most widely used. Most anyone who has spent much time at all on the web has seen a banner ad, which tend to be small rectangular ads that sit in various spots around a page. Locations are typically on one side or at the bottom (and sometimes top) of the page.

The banner ad might be the oldest and least sexy of all the types of web ads, but it shares a common purpose with all web ads. All web ads are designed to get the viewer to click on them in order to give them more information or push them further down the sales cycle. The banner ad resembles the traditional print ad in many ways, but differs in one important respect. And the banner ad, like all web ads, contains a hyperlink which activates when the view clicks on the ad. The hyperlink then sends the viewer to a new page.

Banner ads are found in a variety of sizes, though the shape of most is either square or rectangle. There are, officially, eight different banner sizes, as determined by their pixel dimensions. What's called a full banner ad is 468 x 60 pixels and is the size of a banner that is most widely used.

Beyond that, there is a great deal of variability in the actual creative content of the ads themselves. Initially banner ads were limited to text that was mostly static and sometimes rotated. Today banner ads are much more graphically rich, though they the simple ones are typically confined to one static GIF of JPEG image. Animated and graphically enhanced banners are also used, as are banners that employ audio and video features.

Banners ads were the firsts on the block of web advertisement, and they remain a mainstay to this day. They play important function for advertisers in helping to easily drive would-be buyers further down the process. They are also today used at times at part of a larger package of ads that includes pop-ups, floaters and even television ads.

DIFFERENT WEB ADS SERVE DIFFERENT PURPOSES

Website advertising has boomed as a business in the past several years. Advertising on the web was initially relegated to a banner ad or two, and was, compared to today, very expensive. The cost of advertising on the web was part of the initial resistance to the channel from companies in the early years, because they could not justify the cost against expected returns. As companies stayed away from web ads in droves, and as new ways of pricing the ad space came into practice, pricing came down, opening the door to what is now the fastest growing segment of the ad world.

Web ads are particularly suited to direct response ad methodologies. Direct response seeks to get viewers/readers to perform a specific act, from returning a postcard, to calling a toll-free number, to requesting a download to making a purchase. The classic example of the direct response ad is the phrase: "Act Now!"

The web is useful for this purpose because the media is inherently interactive, and because the cost of transferring information needed to make a purchase is relatively low. Though an advertiser must pay for the cost of the ad, once the viewer clicks on the ad they are taken to a place (the advertiser's site, typically) where the cost of providing all the information necessary is very low and spread across many different buyers and potential buyers.

So, let's say that you sell phones and you want to advertise on the web. You do your research to find the right place to put the ad, and then you do the placement. The cost of that ad is bounded by the amount of traffic it gets, and you will have a general idea of this from the start.

But once a potential buyer clicks the ad, he is taken to your site, where you have virtually unlimited space to introduce all the phones and their various features and limitations. Traditional print ads do not facilitate this process as readily because there is an additional step readers must go through; they must put down the newspaper and magazine and go to their computer and pull up your website.

The web offers other advantages for advertiser as well, through more targets ads. Direct response advertising has been with us for many years and has found a new and more spacious home on the web, indicating that the growth we've seen in web ads is likely to continue.

HOW TO CREATE AN EFFECTIVE BANNER AD

Banner ads are the backbone of the internet ad world. While there are no hard and fast rules about what makes for a more successful banner ad, there are some general guidelines that will help you maximize the investment you are placing in creating and placing these ads. For some people, they will find just the right ad out of the gate, which will drive traffic to their site and help increase revenue. But most of us are not that fortunate. Or good.

Even many experienced advertisers run through a trial and error process with the banner ads that they run. One of the great advantages of web advertising is that its effectiveness can be measured quickly and precisely, so it does not take long to determine how effective an ad is. That said, you want to minimize as much as possible inefficient ad spends, so it helps to try and shorten that trial and error process as much as possible.

So, there are a few guidelines that can help you get started. First, know that where – on what type of site – you place the ad matters. Probably more than any other factor. You want to make sure that your ad is being seen by as many people as possible who are likely to buy your product. Along the same lines, where on the page your ad appears also matters. Ads that fall below the bottom of the first page are generally less likely to be successful than those that placed in the upper and middle right hand side of the page.

Next, make sure the ad itself is asking something of the viewer. It should be as specific as possible and it should be as related to a direct sale as possible. In other words, the banners should point to products and services rather than just your website in general. And in that same vein, when you create the link from the banner ad, make sure that it goes to the particular place on your web site where someone needs to be to buy your product. The link should not go to the home page.

Banners are not large, and the messages that go in them should also be very brief. Two or three words is best. And use images that are interesting and relevant to your product or service.

People should be intrigued by the image, but not confused.

WHAT TO LOOK FOR IN SITES WHERE YOU WANT TO ADVERTISE

When you are first launching into the world of advertising on the web, you will want to make sure you do some front end research in order to get maximum leverage of your advertising dollars. Not all sites are made alike. Not even close. And there are a number of things you can look for in the site to help you determine whether or not it is the right site for you to pour your important marketing dollars into.

First of all, make an inventory of the types of websites where you customers are likely to visit. Most products and services are purchased by people from a wide range of walks of life, but there tend also to be shared characteristics among purchasers of different goods and services. The more specific you can match the web site with the interests and activities of your buyers, the more likely you are to ultimately capture their interest with your ad and drive toward a purchase.

Second, avoid the trap of feeling like you have to be everywhere all the big players are. Sometimes, your larger competitors or the bigger companies have good reason for being where they are and that reason may not apply to your business. Second, larger companies have bigger budgets, so they can afford to experiment in different markets and accept a lower rate of return in a secondary market. While it might be alluring to try and run with the big dogs, it's not always the smartest strategy.

Next, compare costs. Different websites have different cost structures. Expect to pay more for sites that generate a lot of traffic and less in those cases where traffic is lighter. Also expect to pay a premium for a site that appeals to a narrow range that is part of an attractive demographic (such as high net worth individuals). These sites can commend higher prices because the buyers that they attract with their content fit a highly desirable category.

Don't forget to look at the ad itself. It should be clear, interesting, placed in the upper part of the screen.

Finally, make sure that your own website is in order before you start buying and placing ads. It might be tempting to go out and get the ads going so you can drive traffic, but if you sites is not prepared, you will end up shooting yourself in the foot.

WHAT'S UP NEXT FOR ADVERTISING ON THE WEB

Click-through rates, which determine the effectiveness of web based ads, have been falling in the past several years, one indication that their effectiveness as a tool for driving sales revenue, has declined. And many have said that the days of banner ads on the web are numbered. On the other hand, there are some in the industry who think the best days of banner ads are still in front of them.

Whatever the case, the web as an advertising channel is not going away any time soon. The newer ads, like pop ups are finding both applause and criticism. Some find them nothing but annoyance, because you have to close them in order to view content. On this basis, some people actually boycott companies that advertise in the fashion, as they consider it a rude, ham-fisted intrusion on their right to view content without interruption.

There are some new additions to the web ad scene as well, and these also bear watching. One such newcomer is the interstitial ad. These ads load before the web page and automatically disappear before the page finishes loading. They are, thus, considered to be somewhat less intrusive. Typically a banner ad that mirrors the interstitial ad will appear on the page after it is finished loading. In this way, those who use them can insure that the any interest generated by them is not lost to someone who did not react quickly enough to click on them.

The arrival of television ads on the web has also been an evolutionary step in the art of web based advertising. These ads very closely replicate ads you would see on television. They are produced around vignettes, and have both audio and video as they run. These spots do not run as long as typical TV ads, but they thus far have been viewed as being very effective by the advertisers who run them.

In many respects, we have only just begun to tap the surface of the web's potential as an ad channel. For as widespread as internet use is around the world, there are still hundreds of millions of people who are not yet connected to the web. And the inventiveness of how ads appear and interact with users is still in the developing phase.

As the programming underlying these ads improves and as more people move to the web

SELLING AD SPACE ON THE WEB

It is no secret that the web is a great place to advertise. Ads can be more easily directed to target demographics, they are typically cost-effective, and their effectiveness in driving sales behaviors can be readily and fully tracked and measured. So, many advertisers have shifted increasing amounts of their ad budgets to the web. For those who own spaces that would like to sell advertising space, this shift has been welcome.

That said, selling ad space does require some forethought and benefits from following some established pathways. Those starting out might wish to join a banner ad network. These networks provide the service of attracting advertisers, and monitoring the success of the ads in addition to helping you find the right placement of ads on your site. While these networks do offer these significant advantages, they do so a price. They typically take a substantial portion of the ad revenue generated by the site.

The networks also will be selective in who they work with, so it is good to anticipate this as well. They look for high traffic sites, those with a couple hundred thousand visitors per month or more. There are additional options for those with less traffic, including a CPM program or a click-through program. The trade off is in the expected revenue, which will be lower. However, if your site is not heavily trafficked enough, this might well be the best way to get started.

You can also consider selling the space yourself. This is not a bad way to go if your site is heavily trafficked enough to generate interest from advertisers. Advertisers do have the upper hand in this respect; there are fewer advertisers than there are sites for them to place their ads, so the market is competitive. In order to build a case for your site with advertisers, you will need to show them your traffic numbers as well as any information on steps you are taking to keep traffic levels high and growing. You might need to weight the costs of providing ad space at initially lower rates to attract buyers with the idea of building loyalty over time.

Attracting some brand name advertisers to your site, even if you have to reduce rates a little to do so, will help to convince other advertisers of the value of your site, so there might be a good justification for flexibility on price.

A RUN-DOWN OF THE TYPES OF WEB-BASED ADS

Not all ads are created alike, whether those ads are appearing in a magazine, newspaper, or on a bulletin board or television. Different types of ads are designed to create different effects, attract different types of responses and elicit different types of behavior. This is no less so the case with ads that appear on the web. The web has undergone a transformation where advertising is concerned and today the state of web-based ads is light years from where it started.

Following is a run-down of different types of ads and their various features.

Banner ads are the classic type of web ad. They tend to be static (or include rolling text or images), and they occupy one space on the web pages. The aim of the banner ad is simply to project a message and get the viewer to click on it for more information or the next step of the sales process. Sidebar ads sit along one vertical axis of the page. They are larger – about two times larger – than banner ads, and they have the chief advantage of never leaving the page. As the viewer scrolls down the page, so does the ad. These ads are also more expensive than traditional banner ads.

Pop-up ads open in a separate page, typically on top of the content the viewer is trying to see. These ads, which many people find annoying, are meant to be intrusive and to force the viewer to act to either follow the ad's link or cancel the ad.

Floating ads are a little like pop-ups only they are designed to be a little more visually clever. Their images often float out of the copy and then move off the page. These ads can be twice as effective as static ads in getting viewers to click on them.

Television ads. These ads look, act and run very much like ads you see on television. They have vignettes, complete with action and audio, and they are providing to be highly effective in promoting the desired viewer behavior.

All of these ads can be run separately or in combination. Some advertisers like to run both a television or floating ad and have related static ads running alongside the same page after the animated ads leave the page. It remains to be seen what the next generation of web based ads will look like, but one thing is certain. Advertisers love working with the web as a channel.

They have better control over their costs and the effectiveness of the ad, and with new forms of ads coming on line, they increasingly have more creative control as well.

BUYING AND SELLING WEB-BASED ADVERTISING

Buying and selling advertising on the web hold some important differences from buying and selling advertising space in other venues.

In terms of buying ad space, you can simply contact the owners of the web site where you are interested, and this is a good solution if you there are only a couple of potential sites where you wish to get placements. If you have a big list of sites, this can be a time-consuming method. The costs you can expect will vary based on the amount of traffic the site receives, and will range from about $5 to more than $100 for every 1000 impressions.

If your ad plans are more complex and you are spending a lot on the ad campaign, you can think about getting an ad agency to do the work. They will find the right sites, negotiate the best deals and do the placements. You can also join what's call a banner ad network, which is broker that works with both publishers and advertisers. They perform the function of placing banner ads tracking performance.

On the other hand selling ad space can also be done in a number of different ways. First, you can sell the space yourself, which is a good way to consider if your site is busy enough to generate advertiser interest. You might need to weight the costs of providing ad space at initially lower rates to attract buyers with the idea of building loyalty over time if your site is not heavily trafficked.

Those just starting out in the world of ad selling want to consider a banner ad network. These networks attract advertisers, and monitor the success of the ads in addition to helping you find the right placement of ads on your site. While these networks do offer these significant advantages, they do so at a price, which is typically pretty high. They are also selective; they want to work with sites that are highly trafficked. Generally, the larger networks look for sites with couple hundred thousand visitors per month or more. There are additional options for those with less heavily trafficked sites, including either a CPM program or a click-through program.

The trade off is in the expected revenue, which will be lower. However, if your site is not heavily trafficked enough, this might well be the best way to get started.

BANNER ADS VS OTHER TYPES OF ADS

When you are first trying to get your arms around web advertising, the range of options and the implications of your choices can be difficult to sort through. One of the key questions you will have to ask from the start is what type of ad you want to place. There is nothing to say that you have to limit your choice to one type or another, because many are often used in concert with others. But it is a good idea to know be able to make a determination about what kind of effect you expect to get as compared to the amount of money you will be spending on the ad.

Banner ads are the classic type of web based ad. They come in a variety of sizes and shapes, and are designed primarily to drive direct response sales success. Not particularly well suited for branding messages, rather banner ads are good for getting the attention of a potential buyer and incenting them to click and be brought to your site. Once on your site, you have near unlimited space to get their interest and help drive them further down the sales path. With these ads, remember to keep the message simple, the image relevant and the link on the banner directed to the place on your site where buyers need to be (not the home page). And keep the ads specific.

Skyscraper ads run vertically up and down one side of the page and are preferable to banners in that they never leave the site of the pager viewer, because as the viewer scrolls down, so does the ad. Beyond that, these ads work in very similar ways to banner ads.

Pop up ad are also effective for getting the attention of viewers, and not always the best kind of attention. Pop ups are designed to intrude on the copy and require viewers to take an action to remove them (or follow them). They are similar to "fly over" ads which appear after the page is loaded and then fly over the page after they have sent their message. These last two types of ads are a little more effective at driving people who seller websites.

Finally, some companies use a combination of these types of ads, in particular when they have adopted a "take over" strategy, in which they inundate a site with their ads to exclusion of other ads.

THE WEB ALL ADVERTISING ALL THE TIME

For those who have been dismayed by the trend toward greater infiltration of the web by advertising, the future is not looking any brighter. In fact, the trend is toward ever increasing, some would say ever intrusive, forms and placements of ads on the web. Pop-up ads and floating ads and the newest twist: television ads have all been making their way in greater numbers to web pages everywhere.

And there are evolving ad strategies that are contributing to the trend toward greater pervasiveness of web ads. Some companies have begun producing what they call "takeover" campaigns, which are designed to take over a web site and cover it with their advertising messages. One other approach is similar. It is a multiple web ad approach that blankets a page or a portion of a site with different types of ads.

The advertiser might, under this approach, buy multiple banner and sidebars ads, two or three pop up ads and a floating ad. (A cornucopia of intrusion in the minds of some). All of these ads would be supplanted by a television ad. Television ads, for those new to the term, run and act just like regular television ads. The feature vignettes, motion and audio. But they have the added advantage of allowing viewers to click on the ad to learn more or make a purchase.

Companies that have traditionally funneled significant portions of their ad revenues to television are moving in increasing numbers to the web because of this added advantage. It is not possible to get a television viewer to push the dial on the remote to get more information (at least this technology is not currently widely available), so the web's ability to facilitate further conversation with a potential buyer is a tremendous advantage in the minds of advertisers.

Perhaps the good news in all of this is that there are limits to how much advertising can go on a web page, both physical in terms of the page dimensions and psychological in terms of the viewers ability to tolerate and absorb the messages. At some point, where there are too many messages, people will just tune them out and not be able to absorb them. Where that point lies is a matter for debate between social scientists, advertisers and the web sites that gain their revenue through advertising dollars. Stay tuned for more.

THE EVOLUTION OF WEB-BASED ADVERTISING

There is no doubt left as to whether the web will remain as a powerful channel for sending out advertising messages to the masses. Usage of the web continues to grow and more new internet users come online every day. And the state of the art of the technology that lies underneath web ads continues to become more sophisticated, making the use of the web increasingly effective and efficient in driving marketing results.

What was one thought of as completely inappropriate space to put advertising has been perhaps the most successful development in the ad world since the development of the printing press and the invention of the television. The growth in web-based ads is accounted for by several developments, but the most important two are that web ads are more targeted and they are today more cost effective than most any other types of mass market ad spending.

As a result, web ads more and more advertisers are jumping on the bandwagon, and not just the traditional large budget ad spenders. As the web has helped to level the playing field in so many areas of life, it has also helped to make the process of getting attention for products and services more attainable to the small businesses and low budget ad spenders out there as well.

The ads are particularly attractive for small budget folks because they tend to drive short-term action. They are in other words perfect for the purpose of direct response ads. Direct response advertising has been the mainstay of companies with limited marketing budgets. The alternative form of marketing, branding, is typically unaffordable for small companies, and the returns on it are typically longer term. They must make their ads spends work in a direct fashion and typically over the very short term.

This trend toward increased use of the web as an ad vehicle has plenty of momentum and that is not likely to change. However, what is becoming increasingly questioned is not just how far ads can go in taking over the attention spaces of the viewers and the content zones of the pages they are trying to view. Ads are becoming increasingly intrusive and there is a question about where the point of diminished returns exists. In other words, how far can you go before viewers start tuning out the messages altogether. There are limits to everything, including how much information we can productively absorb; it could be we are approaching those limits today.

DIFFERENT WEB ADS SERVE DIFFERENT PURPOSES

The web is grown tremendous as an adverting channel in the past decade. There is very little that is advertised in the traditional channels that is not also advertised on the web these days. Cars, legal services, toothpaste and dog treats, cereal and fine dining establishments all pay to advertise on the web.

If you are looking to market a product or service these days, you are probably evaluating the various pros and cons of advertising on the web. Many traditional advertisers have increasingly more larger portions of their ad budgets to the web, citing its more target nature, and effectiveness as an ad platform. There are various issues to consider when look at advertising on the web, and one of them the type of actual ad you chose to market your product or service.

One type of ad is called the sidebar ad. These ads are also called skyscraper ads, for the way the visual of them looks like a tall building standing on the side of the webpage. A sidebar ad, thus, is vertically oriented, running about 120 pixels wide and as much as 600 pixels high.

Sidebar ads offer a few important advantages, the first of which is their size. They are typically around twice the size of a traditional banner ad, and sometimes larger.

But the other advantage is in the way they "stick" to the page. While you can scroll past a traditional banner ad, you cannot scroll a sidebar ad off of the page. This feature can be a significant advantage, because it means that viewers will have your ad in their range of vision the entire time they are on the page. So while they might initially not notice the ad as their eye searches for the content they are seeking, there is a greater chance that the ad will catch their eye as they scroll down the page.

The tradeoff for the larger size and greater "stickiness" of a side bar ad is there higher cost, relative to a banner ad. Sidebar ads typically have a click-through rate of about 1 percent, which is roughly twice that of a banner ad.

Getting to know the various tradeoffs involved with different types of web ads will help you to determine which type of ads will be the most effective and efficient for your advertising purposes. Sidebar ads can have a lot of advantages, and if the cost is justifiable, may be a great way to get the word out about your offerings.

WEBSITE ADS COMES IN DIFFERENT SHAPES AND SIZES

The range of options available for web site advertising has grown tremendously, alongside the tremendous growth of the web as an ad channel. Gone are the days of the lowly, static banner ad that almost looked like it was trying to not draw too much attention to itself. Today, advertising on the web is starting to much more closely mirror that of television, though advertisers have been somewhat slow in pushing for this.

Because the web was not built as an ad channel, some people initially had very strong negative reactions to the presence of ads. But as time went on, and the power of the vehicle for advertising became very clear, more advertisers took the plunge into web ads. Overtime, web viewers have grown more accustomed to the presence of these ads, although there are still come kinds of ads that inspire out and out anger.

The term pop-up ad has become virtually synonymous with the notion of annoyance. A pop-up ad is one that opens a new screen in front of the screen with the content the viewer is trying to see. Viewers must either click to engage the link or click to cancel the page in order to see their content. Many people absolutely hated these ads when they first came on the scene, and they were not shy about saying so. However, with the passage of time, the anger has subsided and we have grown accustomed, or at least resigned, to them.

In this respect, the web is starting to resemble television, where advertising is completely intrusive, but also nearly universally accepted as a part of the television viewing experience. With growing acceptance of the idea of ads on the web, has come an increasing degree of intrusion of those ads. Now, in addition to the traditional pop-ups, we see floating ads and what look like television ads.

Floating ads usually appear on the page after it is loaded. They can seem to move directly out of the copy and then standstill while the message is being delivered, before floating off or just disappearing from the screen. As would be expected when new elements are added, many people have objected to these floating ads. But they are proving to be twice or three times as effective as traditional web ads, so they are likely to remain on the scene. At least until the next thing comes along.

DEFINING THE OBJECTIVES OF A BANNER AD

Banner ads are the longest standing type of web based ads out there, and the objectives attached to them are well established. There are several objectives with any banner ad. First, advertisers hope that the ads are seen, and thus contribute to the increasing brand awareness of their company and products/services.

Brand building is generally done slowly and over time, so the advertiser anticipates it will take "multiple hits" of a brand message on a potential buyer before an actual purchase is made. The intent of sending a brand message is to place the idea of the company in the mind of the buyer, so that when they do go to make a purchase, that particular brand comes first to mind.

Second, advertisers hope that the banner ads will be clicked on, which will take the would-be buyer to their site, where they have additional space to continue the sales "conversation."

Finally, once potential buyers have clicked-through to the advertisers web site, the hope is that they will buy things. Not all banner ads are meant to result in a direct purchase in this way, but even in the case where they are not, the hope is that the potential customer will "walk away" with some of the company's, for example a download.

The ways in which banners ads are measured against these objectives varies. Generally, advertiser will analyze the number of click throughs produced by an ad. A click through is simply when someone sees the banner and clicks through it to the advertiser's web site. In fact, this is the basis of pricing for many ads, cost increases with each click through. Related to this is the click through rate, which is simply a ratio of the number times click through occur compared to the number of times the page is viewed.

Advertisers also look at page views, or the number of times the pages are accessed by viewers. This number is indicative of the potential size of the market available to the advertiser. Ad space is also sold in this way, by the number of impression a page receives.

Advertisers also look at the cost of sale, or the amount of money they spent on the ad versus the amount of money in revenue was produced by that ad. This is one of the great advantages of web based ads; they allow for easy and direct tracking of the effectiveness of the ad itself.

BUYING ADVERTISING SPACE ON THE WEB

For the first time advertiser on the web, approaching the process can be a bit daunting. There are good reasons to advertise on the web, and if your are consider the web as a channel for your ads, you've no doubt heard about them. Web ads are more targeted and can tend to be a little more cost-effective than traditional forms of advertising.

There are various alternatives for how to go about the process. For starters, you can simply talk with the owners of the web site where you think you might want to place ads. If you have identified only a couple of potential sites for your ad dollars, this can be a good solution, but if you are looking to do a broad campaign it can be a time-consuming way to go. If you do go this route, make sure you get all the critical information from them, such as how well their content fits your demographic, the options they have available for placement and costs. You will also want to learn about each site's particular process for submitting ads. Many sites post this information on the site itself, but if not, you can call or write for the information.

The costs you can anticipate will vary based on the amount of traffic the site receives. Cost will range from as low as $5 (perhaps less) to more than $100 for every 1000 impressions on the site. The main driver of cost is the amount of traffic a site receives, but some sites, those that cater to coveted niche markets, will charge a premium for access to their base.

If you have ad plans that are at all complex, or you are devoting significant dollars to the ad campaign, you can also consider higher an ad agency to do the work of finding the right sites, negotiating the best deals and doing the placements. Ad agencies are a great way to go in many respects. Because this is their business they can help you get the greatest leverage out of your ad spend. You will, of course, be charged for their services, so using an ad agency only makes sense with budgets of a certain size; also many agencies have budget minimums that they will work with.

You can also consider joining a banner ad network. Banner ad networks perform the function of a broker that works with both publishers and advertisers. They take on the role of placing the banner ads and keeping tabs on the performance of those ads.

KNOW YOUR OPTIONS FOR WEB BASED ADS

Different types of ads have different objectives and create various effects, while attracting different types of responses and eliciting different types of behavior. So, knowing the differences between them can help you to determine which type of ad is best for your situation and advertising needs.

Following is a brief overview of the various types of ads and the features associated with them.

Banner ads are typically what we think of when we think about ads on the web. They are typically static (or include rolling text or images), and they sit in one place on a web page (as opposed to moving around, like other types of ads) The objective of a banner ad is to get out a message that prompts the viewer to click on it for more information about your product or service. In this way, they potential buyer is moved further down the sales process.

Sidebar are a special form of banner ad. They sit along one vertical axis of the page and run the height of the page, which is where they got their nickname "skyscraper ads." They are about two times larger than typical banner ads, and they have the unique advantage of never leaving the page, no matter how far down the viewer scrolls. Like banners, these ads are built to get people to click on them, an act that will send the viewer to the advertiser's website, where more information will be provide. Because of their size, sidebar ads are usually more expensive than banners.

Pop-up ads are another type of ad. They open in a separate page, typically on top of the content the viewer is trying to see. These ads, which many people find annoying, are meant to be intrusive and to force the viewer to act to either follow the ad's link or cancel the ad.

Floating ads are a little like pop-ups only they are designed to be a little more visually clever. Their images often float out of the copy and then move off the page. These ads can be twice as effective as static ads in getting viewers to click on them.

"Television" ads are yet another form. They look and behave, very much like ads you see on television. They feature little stories, run with action and audio, and they are proving to be highly effective in promoting the desired viewer behavior.

INTRODUCING TELEVISION COMMERCIALS TO THE WEB

When television first began to take hold of the American imagination and set up permanent residence in American homes, commercials were part of the deal. In fact, some of the most enduring television shows in history started as vehicles to sell products. Daytime soap operas as they were called from the early years were conceived of as programs that would be attractive to stay at home wives, who were the target market for a variety of soap and laundry detergent products.

The web was a little different. The early days of the web were marked by the openness of the platform, its potential for universal reach and its appeal as a haven from commercialization. That didn't last long. Initially companies set up web sites that looked very much like brochure, and then very quickly advertising came on the scene. The reaction was not entirely positive, but the die was cast, as the Internet boom of the 1990s was fueled by the media potential of the web.

Since that time we have seen the state of the art of web advertising shift from static banner ads, to sidebar ads that never leave the page, to pop up ads that sit on top of the content that viewers wish to see. This latter type of ad would be akin to a twenty-second commercial appearing on top of a television show that continues to run. And the reaction, again, has not been entirely positive.

But this has not stopped the onward march toward new forms and fashions of marketing on the web. The most recent example of these ads look very much like television commercials. They appear on the side of the page as it loads – and sometimes on top of the page – and they are animated. The ads are also sometimes created like audio, and feature vignettes that are selling a product or service of some kind. They, in other words, are just like television commercials.

In addition to being powerful branding devices, these ads provide an advantage that traditional television advertising cannot. These ads can allow viewers to immediately click to learn more or make a purchase. As such, the web-based television ads provide the advertiser the opportunity to have something of an ongoing discussion with the potential buyer in a way that a TV ad cannot. While TVs can direct viewers about how to behave next, the viewers must take the additional step of picking up the phone or going to the store, etc. With a web TV, viewers simply need to click to go to the next stage of the sales process.

A SHORT HISTORY OF A BOLD MEDIA

When advertising first started appearing on the world wide web, there were many critics should argued that it would never be accepted by web users and would turn out to be a huge waste of money for advertisers. Though those who disagreed saw huge potential in the net as a way of delivering ads in a new way, those who argued against it said that there would never be enough viewership to justify it.

Of course, that proved to be very wrong very quickly. The pace of adaption of the web far outstripped the telephone, the radio and television. Within a few short years, significant portions of the nation's population were wired up and connected to the net. Within a few short years after that, we began to see the precipitous decline in the health of some of the major traditional media outlets, like newspapers and magazines. Even television advertising was not unaffected by the growth in the web based model.

Web advertisers very quickly saw how the platform would help them a couple of very important things. One is that the web as a medium allows users to make quick on the spot decisions about whether to follow an ad and eventually make a purchase or not. Second, is that the technology behind web ads allows advertisers to rate the effectiveness of their ads more quickly and thoroughly than ever before.

The second aspects provides a huge advantage in that it allows ad buyers to determine where they need to makes shifts in their ad strategies in order to maximize their spends. In the past, that information could take weeks or months to obtain for newspaper and magazine advertising, and even then the information about how effective the ads were was less than complete, compared to what is offered on the web based platform.

As the technology and art form began to develop, we began to see increasing numbers of traditional advertisers begin to look at the web in a way they had not before. Those who were tentative about approaching the web for their ads soon lost their fear and joined in as well. Now it is hard to imagine a single product or service category that is not in some way advertised on the web.

The web has also brought a more level playing field to smaller businesses, many of whom could never afford the traditional advertising rates.

WEBSITE ADVERTISING'S BRIEF HISTORY INCLUDES RAPID EVOLUTIONS

Print forms of advertising have been us with since print forms of communication have been with us. Hundreds of years. Over that time, slow changes have occurred as the commercial side of print publication of newspapers and magazines matured and publishers became increasingly sophisticated about the advertising side of their business. In the early years of newspapers and magazines, for the most part, the publications existed as a way to share news or information, and advertising was how the bills produced by creating the content were paid and profits made.

When advertising first came to web, it did so tentatively. Small banner ads were the first to appear on the occasional web page. The ads were relatively small and initially static and as such they mirrored newspaper ads. Soon after these ads began to appear with animated text, and at times, rotating images. But even these splashier ads were in relatively short supply compared today.

Today it is not unusual to find pages that are twenty to thirty percent covered in ads. And it is not unusual to finds pages filled with pop-up ads and ads that sit on the top of content. This latter type is perhaps the first type of ad that needs to be physically acted upon (canceled or clicked on) in order for the content to be viewable. This new type of ad has been both applauded for its inventiveness and criticized for its intrusiveness.

This new type of ad is emblematic of the changes that web based advertising have brought with them as they have continued to evolve from the early days of the net. Whereas in the past, journals were created to disseminate information, with ads providing the revenue, today sites are created as a platform for advertising and the content is published as means of attracting interest to the ads. Though certainly many content sites exist to provide news and information, the advent of sites that use content as a way to drive ad traffic is a relatively new development in the history of advertising.

It remains to be seen what develops next in the ongoing evolution of web advertising. Some complain that the web has gone too far, and the inundation of marketing on the web has left viewers overwhelmed with too many messages. But advertising has long been the target of complaints, and so far the complaints has done little to slow the pace of its development.

HOW THE WEB REINVIGORATED ADVERTISING

Advertising is nothing new to the world. Attaching sales messages that many people don't care to read or view on to things they want to or must read or view has been a tactic of sales people since for eons. Since the earliest days of advertising very little of substance has changed in this respect. Ads attached to important material or put in places where people cannot avoid seeing them (billboards, train stations, airports) still rules the day in the ad world.

But what has made a material difference in this universe has been the growth of the web. What the web can do that other forms of advertising cannot essentially amounts to leaving the web as the superior way to get highly targeted and thus cost-effective sales messages out to the public. Whereas an ad in a train station will be seen by a very wide demographic (a lot of different types of people ride the train, and they tend to buy a lot of different types of things), web pages tend to be viewed by people looking specifically for the material on that web page.

What lies on that web page likely has some bearing on the demographic characteristics of the viewer, and thus an advertiser can "know" something about the people who are likely to visit the page before they put their ads on it.

Advertising came to the web slowly and tentatively. But the pace of change has been pretty rapid. Where once you would find one or perhaps two banner ads on a page, today you will find about one-fifth of the page covered, if not more, in ads. And unlike with newspapers and magazines, these ads do not only sit alongside content. Web pages today are filled with ads that sit on top of, or otherwise obscure the content of the page.

Now this is something new in the world. And not everyone is happy about it. Many people object to the notion of ads at all, but even the more tolerant among us are objecting to the ad become a barrier to reading the content on the page.

Of course, who only knows where we go from here. The next developments in web advertising are just as likely to be more controversial than less so. With such a highly targeted forum advertisers and the web sites they support are having a hard time turning their backs on the opportunity to get the attention of would-be buyers.

WEBSITE ADVERTISING CONTINUING TO EVOLVE

There is no question but that the presence that advertising has had within the web environment has expanded tremendously in recent years. What used to be thought of a little more than a static banner ad opportunity, the web today is exploding with ever more plentiful, animated, and sometimes intrusive ads.

The trend is due to several factors. One is that the barriers to the web as an accepted place for advertising have vanished almost completely. There are few products or service types that are not marketed on the web today. The other is that the web has become the fastest growing advertising outlet available, and use of it is increasing.

Both of these trends point to the same net result, which is that ads are plentiful on the web, and there needs to be a way for each to distinguish itself from the next in the mind of the page view. As a result, more ads are appearing as animated, and active. Some are even designed to initiate after the viewer has already started reading a page.

These ads share one other thing in common: the page viewer must take a direct action to remove them from the page (and typically what they are trying to read on the page). Viewers must either click on the ad to engage it, or they must close it out.

For those who wonder why there now seem to be so many more ads than before and who seem to feel more encroached upon by those ads, know that you are not alone and your observations are not just your own. As ads become ever more pervasive and ever more intrusive, viewers become ever more put upon by them. So, advertisers and the sites that serve them are playing a game of chicken with viewers. Web site advertising is believed to be among the most effective of the available forms of advertising, but it is wearing thin the patience of viewers everywhere.

The overall trend toward greater use of the web as an ad vehicle is unquestioned, but what is becoming increasingly in doubt is not just the limits of viewers' patience, but of their attention. One trailing implication of the onslaught of all of this intrusive advertising is whether or not it undercuts the web as an effective vehicle by overloading the attention spans of viewers.

There are limits to everything, including how much information we can productively absorb, and some would argue that the current state of web advertising is pushing those limits.

THE FUTURE OF WEBSITE ADVERTISING

Considering how quickly the website advertising industries have grown up in the past several years, it is daunting to think about how much more they can possibly evolve. Web advertising has massively changed the face of advertising as a marketing strategy, and you need look no further than the massive flow of funds into web sites that sell space, and away from traditional print media to see how impressively this has happened. But print media is not the only form that is being changed by web ads.

Television is facing its own threat from the web platform, something that only a few years ago, many thought was not likely. The web was seen as a good place for static ads, but not the kind of dynamic ads that are seen on television. One of the major hurdles to television ads on the web was seen as the way that the web does not have a natural place for these audio and video enabled ads. Television, of course, does. In fact the whole production of a television show, newcast, etc is built around the requirements for the advertising that supports them.

On the web, there was thought to be no natural place for a TV ad to be placed. But we have found a way around that: we simply interrupt programming, in effect. Most TV ads load right after the page has finished loading, and many find a way to somehow obscure or block the content while they run. These ads are designed, typically, to be shorter than the average television commercial, but they are definitely getting seen.

As a result, more companies are moving increasing proportions of their television ad spends to the web as well. In addition to being extremely effective powerful branding devices (in part because they are new), these ads provide an advantage that traditional television advertising cannot. Web-based television ads will allow viewers to immediately click to learn more or make a purchase. As such, the web-based television ads provide the advertiser the opportunity to have something of an ongoing discussion with the potential buyer in a way that a TV ad cannot. The effectiveness of web based television ads, just like with any web based ad, can also be measured in virtual real-time, so advertisers can adjust the ads or the placement of them in order to maximize their effectiveness.